NBRANs

# A Dog's Journey Home

*25 Stories of Rescue and Fostering*

BRENDA COOPER

Copyright ©2022
Brenda Cooper
NBRANs A Dog's Journey Home
25 Stories of Rescue and Fostering
All rights reserved.

No part of this publication may be reproduced, distributed, or transmitted in any form or by any means, including photocopying, recording, or other electronic or mechanical method without the prior written permission of the author, except in the case of brief quotations embodied in critical reviews and certain other non-commercial uses permitted by copyright law.

Brenda Cooper
National Brittany Rescue & Adoption Network

Printed in the United States of America
First Printing 2022
First Edition 2022

LCCN: 2022910844
Paperback ISBN: 979-8-9863951-0-4
10 9 8 7 6 5 4 3 2 1

This book contains real and true stories depicted by foster families within the NBRAN organization.

All rights reserved worldwide. Because of the dynamic nature of the internet, any web addresses or links contained in this book may have changed since publication and may no longer be valid.

Editors: Brenda Cooper and Michele Moyer
www.nbran.org

## Dedication

This book is dedicated to all the Brittanys that NBRAN has rescued and the ones we have yet to meet. Each one of these spirited dogs has a story. Some stories we know while others remain a mystery. Either way, the dogs that enter our rescue family all have one thing in common - they are now safe, and we will work hard to make sure they are loved for whatever time they have left.

We'd also like to dedicate this book in memory of our friend Gaye Bricker.

# Table of Contents

Acknowledgements .................................................................... 1
Foreword ................................................................................... 3
Chapter 1 ................................................................................... 5
   *Love Like A Hurricane*
Chapter 2 ................................................................................... 8
   *Failing Never Felt So Good*
Chapter 3 ................................................................................. 13
   *The One That Started It All*
Chapter 4 ................................................................................. 16
   *Tiny Dancer and the Time Keeper*
Chapter 5 ................................................................................. 19
   *The Tale of Slim and Sassy*
Chapter 6 ................................................................................. 23
   *A Little Roan Dog Named Tucker*
Chapter 7 ................................................................................. 27
   *MVP Mable*

Chapter 8 .................................................................................................... 30
   *Sweet Dot*
Chapter 9 .................................................................................................... 32
   *Our Chiefy*
Chapter 10 .................................................................................................. 35
   *Sweet to the Very End*
Chapter 11 .................................................................................................. 37
   *Buster*
Chapter 12 .................................................................................................. 41
   *Maddie's Chair*
Chapter 13 .................................................................................................. 45
   *Perfect Max*
Chapter 14 .................................................................................................. 50
   *Half-Brother Surprise*
Chapter 15 .................................................................................................. 53
   *Never Say Never*
Chapter 16 .................................................................................................. 56
   *Bernie's Journey*

Chapter 17 ..................................................................................... 59
  *Bear's Purpose*
Chapter 18 ..................................................................................... 63
  *Daddy's Girl*
Chapter 19 ..................................................................................... 67
  *1,279 Days*
Chapter 20 ..................................................................................... 71
  *Ellie's Story*
Chapter 21 ..................................................................................... 75
  *Bandit the Heart Stealer*
Chapter 22 ..................................................................................... 79
  *Brave Brady*
Chapter 23 ..................................................................................... 84
  *The Tale of Two Ellies*
Chapter 24 ..................................................................................... 89
  *Lady*
Chapter 25 ..................................................................................... 93
  *The Joy of Fostering*

## Acknowledgements

Foster Homes – The work you do is invaluable. You are the frontline workers that open your hearts and home to each Brittany that comes through our rescue organization. It's hard to find words that are sufficient in showing our appreciation for your tireless effort, compassion, and love. Thank you for the time, attention, and energy you put into sharing your stories for this book, and a heartfelt thanks for all you do for each Brittany that comes through your home.

Board Members, Regional Directors, and State/Provincial Coordinators – NBRAN would not exist without these hardworking and dedicated individuals. These teams support one another with all the moving parts of rescue. This entire group is vital, and they all play a crucial role in our organization, and we are so grateful for their tireless effort and commitment.

Volunteers – We have around 575 volunteers that make up the NBRAN organization. There are volunteer roles that are on the front lines with the dogs while others work behind the scenes in a supportive and collaborative role. Every volunteer plays a part in our rescue operation, and we are grateful for the compassion, sacrifice, and effort each person gives.

Editors – A big thank you to Brenda Cooper and Michele Moyer for your keen eye, dedicated time, and effort in editing this book. Giving forward motion to your giftedness and passion has helped this book reach new heights, and we are grateful to you both for helping us achieve this dream.

Author – Brenda Cooper is a Christian author, volunteer, and supporter of NBRAN. We can't thank her enough for taking her passion and talent and putting it to use with writing this book. She worked alongside each foster to highlight and share their stories and to give a voice to the work that is done. Brenda led the efforts in authoring these stories and in publishing this book to completion, and we can't thank her enough for her time and effort.

# Foreword

As the President of NBRAN I'm honored that we were able to put this book together to share these amazing foster stories. Fostering dogs is a vital part of canine rescue and at NBRAN, it's the safe place for each one until they find their forever home.

Our foster community plays an integral role in providing care and love while a Brittany is in transition. We have 175 foster homes throughout the country and are always adding new ones to our organization. Simply put, we could not do what we do without the support and dedicated effort of each foster family.

Our fosters make sure each Brittany gets the medical attention they need while giving them the lap time and snuggles they deserve. They are the kitchen staff, bathroom attendant, and tug-of-war partner along with the boo-boo kisser and chauffer. Our foster families are loyal and dedicated lovers of Brittanys and we are grateful for the love, compassion, and commitment they provide.

Along with dedicated fosters we have 11 board members and regional directors that oversee our state/provincial coordinators. These teams work together to ensure each Brittany that comes through NBRAN has the best chance for a happy life, and they work harmoniously to find the perfect fit with a forever family. We are thankful for the time, effort, and dedication they give to our teams and NBRAN.

On the following pages you will read chapters that highlight Brittanys that have come through our rescue family and that have impacted us. These are heartfelt stories of courage, pain, triumph, and legacies, and we are honored and privileged that we can share them with you.

Dr. Susan Spaid

NBRAN President

# Chapter 1

## Love Like A Hurricane

Foster name: Bailey

Foster nickname: Bae Bae

Foster parent: Carrie Dezio

Foster state: "The Tar Heel State" – North Carolina

Bailey and I had a lot of firsts together. She was my first foster dog and she ended up being my first foster fail too. I decided to become a foster after losing my last Brittany. I was having a difficult time adjusting to my loss so I felt like fostering may be the way to go. I was introduced to this energetic girl named Bailey. She was a two year old orange and white Brittany that had been surrendered. Her previous owner had originally rescued her from terrible living conditions. Bailey had been kept in a crate for most of her young life and was lacking socialization skills. She was heartworm positive, underweight and needed to be spayed. Bailey had also developed severe anxiety and was scared, shy and timid with people. I decided to open my home to this sweet girl. I figured I'd be a short pit-stop for her until NBRAN could find her a home with a big yard. After all, I lived in a townhome and thought she needed a larger space. This is when Mother Nature stepped in and had other plans for Bailey and me.

A week after our introduction and her coming to foster with me, Hurricane Florence hit North Carolina and we were battling wind speeds of 137 mph. The area was hit with rainfall totals of 20" in some areas. It was our first week together and we were not only getting to know each other, but we were also learning how to survive together. Hurricane Florence brought with it $24 billion in damage across three states. What it gave to Bailey and I was a bond that no storm could tear apart. We were without power for an entire week and together we made the best of it. Fortunately, my office had power restored so Bailey was able to go to work with me. This not only gave her the opportunity to interact with new people, but she also had contact with my coworkers' dogs who joined us at the office. The bond we shared during that catastrophic storm is one I will never forget. It was during that storm where Bailey started trusting me. She slowly came out of her shell and started gaining confidence. I watched as this once shy and timid girl grew wings of courage. Florence taught Bailey how to not only survive but to thrive too.

After a few weeks and finally having our power restored, Bailey and I found our groove. I was walking her five times a day to help with her high energy, and she was enjoying all the sniffs and time outdoors. The time with her was helping me deal with my grief, and I was finding joy in introducing Bailey to new things. It didn't take long for me to realize I couldn't give her up. Having her as a foster was just what I needed and I found so much joy watching her flourish. She may have had a rough start in life, but she has found her forever home with me. Bailey has learned to trust and love again, and she has given me something I will never forget: love like a hurricane.

# Chapter 2

## Failing Never Felt So Good

Foster name: Molly

Foster nickname: Mowszer, Molly Muttler, MowMow

Foster parent: Dave, Mary, Michael, and Thomas Voeltz

Foster state: "The Mount Rushmore State" – South Dakota

Over the past 23 years my family and I have fostered nearly 80 dogs. While that seems like a lot, it pales in comparison to other dedicated foster homes in busier states. Fostering is something that just gets in your blood and, just like eating chocolate chip cookies, once you start, it's hard to stop. One thing I always tell new foster homes is to not fall in love with your new house guest. In the dog community we like to call those "foster fails"; people who intend to foster a dog but end up falling in love with them and adopt the dog for themselves. I let them know we will find a great home for their foster, and it will free up a spot for the next dog that needs help. In 2006, against my own advice, we did exactly that. We foster failed.

Her name was Molly. She was an orange and white Brittany that was approximately nine years old and she had a long cute muzzle. She was a quirky girl that had been in a couple different homes and was having a hard time fitting in. We wanted to help her so she joined our family as a foster. At first, she was a bit aloof and nervous. She liked to be by herself but stayed close enough to observe us. Little by little, she began opening up and started to make herself at home. Instead of watching from another room, Molly began sitting in the same room with us. Eventually she made herself at home on our laps. She was starting to blossom and was trusting us more every day.

Molly was not displaying any of the problems the other foster homes noted about her. She had a few idiosyncrasies but those were little things that made Molly who she was. She quickly found her favorite spot on the end of our couch where she'd sit every morning waiting for our son Thomas to wrap her in her favorite blanket. Soon Molly began to participate in family activities. She enjoyed car rides, afternoon walks, and lounging in the warm sun. She settled in nicely and was fitting in and becoming a part of our pack.

After six wonderful months with us, we found out Molly had a potential adopter who lived in Portland. As Molly's coordinator and foster home, we visited with her extensively about Molly and how it might take her some time to adjust to a new home. We told her about her idiosyncrasies and basically tried to talk her out of wanting her. She said she was willing to give it a try so she was approved to adopt. Molly had become one of the family and we were heartbroken she was leaving. We didn't want to fall prey to the failed foster syndrome I had warned others about. We also knew that we wanted to continue fostering other dogs so even though this made us sad, it was time for Molly to leave.

We had relatives who lived in the Portland area, so we volunteered to drive Molly to her new home. We got there and met Molly's new mom and visited for a while and then said our goodbyes. Our hearts were shattered as we drove home and we felt like we had a paw-shaped hole in our heart with Molly's name on it. Little did we know our paths would cross again.

I checked in with Molly's new adopter and my follow-up calls were very discouraging. Molly was acting up and many of the characteristics the previous foster homes noted were being displayed. We couldn't figure out what was going on and why she was having such a hard time adjusting. After three months my family decided to head back for a visit. As soon as we stepped in the door, Molly was elated to see us. We sat down on the kitchen floor and Molly raced back and forth between us. She licked our faces, put her front paws on our shoulders, and whined loudly. We visited for about an hour and discussed ways to help Molly adjust. Thankfully her new mom was willing to try anything. As we left that afternoon, Molly stood at the door wanting to go home with us. It was heartbreaking all over again.

Molly's new mom tried to help her adjust for close to a year, but in the end, Molly just wasn't fitting in. She wasn't settled and was struggling. We wanted what was best for Molly so we all decided she'd return home to us in South Dakota. Through our NBRAN support team, we set up transport for her. Molly's mom, along with selfless volunteers, agreed to drive Molly. We drove three hours to meet them so we could pick up our girl.

When we pulled up we could see immediately that Molly was a different dog. There was a sadness about her. She wasn't the same happy girl she was when we were fostering her. Upon taking her leash, she seemed depressed and detached, not even raising an eye or showing any interest. With her head down, she jumped into our van and plopped down with a heavy sigh. The light in her eyes was gone, and she just looked so unhappy. I started the van and we headed out of the parking lot when suddenly Molly stood up. Her brown nose went into overdrive as she sniffed the air. Molly recognized our scent. She realized it was us. There was an instant change in her demeanor. Her tail started to wag and she began jumping up and down. It was as if we could see her personality change right before our eyes. The black cloud of sadness melted away and a colorful burst of sunshine radiated. There was our Molly girl. She was back. Our younger son Thomas and Molly had a special bond and when she realized he was sitting in the back of the van, she jumped up in his lap and was delighted to see him. They spent the rest of the drive home loving on each other. It was a beautiful reunion and such a special moment for our family.

When we got home, she immediately made herself right at home on the end of our couch where she previously napped. She returned to her old routine of Thomas wrapping her up in her favorite blanket and went back to eating her favorite foods like popcorn and carrots. Her fun-loving personality was back, and we knew the right place for Molly was at home with us. We soon adopted her, and she lived out the rest of her days and years being loved by us. She was settled. She fit in. She was our first foster fail and, let me tell you, failing never felt so good.

# Chapter 3

## The One That Started It All

FOSTER NAME: COOPER

FOSTER NICKNAME: COOP

FOSTER PARENT: JESSICA STEVENSON

FOSTER STATE: "THE PALMETTO STATE" – SOUTH CAROLINA

One night I got a call about a stray dog that was found only 10 minutes from my house. I had always said I'd never foster a dog because I knew I'd probably get too attached. Something in me just knew I had to help this boy. He was a 10 year old orange and white Brittany named Cooper. I picked him up and took him to my vet to be assessed. He was heartworm positive, needed to be neutered and I found out he was deaf.

Cooper was scared to death of people. I was scared because this was a challenging situation, especially for being my first foster. I love a good challenge so I decided the best thing to do was to treat him like he was my own. We had many vet visits together and after three months of treatment, he was finally heartworm free. He was neutered and I worked with him on house breaking and how to live life indoors. As time went on, Cooper learned to trust me, and a strong bond was formed. I watched as this timid, scared boy turned into a goofy and sweet Brittany. I could see him opening up and turning into the dog he was meant to be.

After six months, Cooper was ready for adoption and after one week, the perfect home was found. His new home already had a Brittany and offered him a loving, safe environment. I cried for two weeks straight after dropping him off because I missed him so much. Despite my sadness, I realized how rewarding this experience had been because I was able to see how far Cooper had come. It can be heartbreaking to see the broken ones, but it's so rewarding to see the difference you can make in their lives.

Cooper will always be special to me because he was the one that started it all. He was my first foster and the one that made me fall in love with fostering. Through the years, I've fostered 15 more dogs and it makes it all worth it when you get to see how happy they are. One of the things I love the most is getting updates from their new families and seeing the dog's picture on family Christmas cards along with updates as to how well they have settled in. I once heard that fostering is like a hospital (Paws-pital) for dogs; we get them well and strong enough to move to their very own home one day. I thought that was such a great explanation and I am so proud to be a part of the foster team that helps to nurse these fur babies to health. That is why fostering is such a great experience and I am so grateful I can be a part of it.

# Chapter 4

## Tiny Dancer and the Time Keeper

Foster name: Buckley and Annie

Foster nickname: Tiny Dancer and Annie Pannie

Foster parents: Bunny and Jeff Adams

Foster state: "Volunteer State" – Tennessee

We are Bunny and Jeff Adams and we started fostering for NBRAN in April of 2020. We already have two Brittanys named Betty and Rusty and they have been a wonderful welcoming committee to the fosters we've brought into our home. We are also the proud parents of two foster fails named Buckley and Annie.

Buckley came to us at around six years old and Jeff knew the moment he laid eyes on him that he wanted him to stay. From the history we were given about Buckley, we knew he was a hunter, but Jeff doesn't hunt much anymore. Jeff takes him out into the woods so they can go on adventures together, and

Buck can still get his love for hunting in while keeping an eye out for squirrels and chipmunks. Just like most Brittanys, Buckley loves his meals. He literally dances when we get his food ready so he has earned the nickname of "Tiny Dancer" from us. He has the cute punky hair that liver colored Brittanys often have and he sometimes takes on the characteristics of a rock band member with his flowing locks.

The other foster fail we have is Annie. She is a hospice foster living out her final time with us. Annie is 12 years old and was a physical mess when she arrived. She had a rough go at life before NBRAN saved her. She needed multiple surgeries due to three tumors. We decided the best place for her was with us. She is also dealing with severe arthritis, has thyroid complications, and has a stage four heart murmur but, despite all of her ailments, Annie is incredibly sweet.

I've only heard Annie bark once. As part of her morning routine, she heads outside and immediately throws herself down on her back and rolls around in the grass. It's her morning moment of Zen. She is also the official time keeper for all the dogs in the house, always knowing when it's time for food and meals. She keeps us honest when it comes to breaking treats in half even though she has lost all of her teeth. She still knows how to beg for nibbles by using her soulful eyes and mental telepathy on us. Before going to sleep each night, Annie insists on both of us rubbing her, which we gladly do. Annie is one of those special dogs that has shown us how rewarding it can be to foster. Her life started out rough but when her time comes she will have known love from us and our pack.

Fostering has been our salvation during the days of Covid-19. We recently sent our 18th foster in two short years to their forever home, and it has been such a rewarding experience. It can be hard to see them go, but we constantly remind ourselves that we are not the only ones who can love and keep these dogs safe and happy. We've made many friends through NBRAN, and all of the volunteers that work tirelessly for these dogs. We are grateful for our experience and will continue to open our home to other Brittanys that need love. Tiny Dancer and the Time Keeper have made our family whole, and we are grateful we get to care for them both.

# Chapter 5

## The Tale of Slim and Sassy

Foster names: Slim and Sassy

Foster nicknames: Slim Jim and Sweet Sassy

Foster parents: Pam and Lewis Burson

Foster state: "The Natural State" – Arkansas

This is the tale of a bonded pair named Slim and Sassy. Sassy came to NBRAN as a puppy and was placed with her first owner at the age of 12 weeks. Her new owner expected her to hunt so she was placed in a warm outdoor kennel with another female Brittany. One day I called to check in to see how Sassy was doing, and her owner informed me that both girls had run away. He said they hadn't been seen in over three weeks. I flew into action contacting the local shelters and vets to put out an alert. After a week of worry, I received a phone call from Sassy's owner. He said both girls had come home, and that he no longer wanted Sassy since she wouldn't hunt. We made arrangements, and soon Sassy was back home with me.

About a month prior to Sassy coming back, I started fostering a young male Brittany by the name of Slim Jim. Slim was just that; a long-legged Brittany that was as wild as the wind. He coincidentally was surrendered for the same reasons as Sassy; he wouldn't hunt. His previous owner told me he'd never paid much attention to him, and I could tell this was the case because he was having a hard time socializing with other dogs. He also had a few idiosyncrasies and he constantly ran nervously up and down our fence line. He often withdrew to his crate to be alone. My husband and I worked hard to gain his trust, and eventually he learned that if he came to us he'd get love and attention. He still wasn't bonding well with our other dogs, but that all changed once Sassy arrived.

As soon as Sassy walked in the door she happily introduced herself to the pack. She walked right over to Slim and sat down next to him. He sniffed her and checked her out and then laid down placing his head on her paw. Their bond was instantly formed. This began joyful days of running, chasing, and never leaving each other's side. One of Slim's favorite things to do was to go up to Sassy and bump her with his nose to initiate play. They'd hunt for moles in the backyard, digging trenches together, and rolling in the dirt. Once they were worn out from the yard games, they'd get on the back porch and take a nap together. It was wonderful to see the bond they had formed. Slim became a normal joyful pup; no more pacing the fence line or being nervous. Together they were sweet, crazy, and content Brittany soul mates.

I knew that this bonded pair could not be separated, and I thought it would be a long time before we found the perfect forever home for them both. To our surprise, within two months, an application came in to adopt them together. We went through the normal routine of interviews and home checks so we could make sure it was a great fit for everyone. Soon, they were on their way to their forever home in Ohio. They had a great backyard and overstuffed couches waiting, and they adjusted well to their new environment. Their new parents tell me of all the double snuggles and funny antics of the pair, and how they are still very bonded to this day.

My experience with fostering has taught me that I should follow the lead of these beautiful dogs. They have such a forgiving nature. They have taught me to love the not-so-perfect people. They have taught me to follow God's lead in how we should love and forgive those that have hurt us. I am so glad I can be a part of their stories in helping them escape their past and loving them into their beautiful future. It is a very rewarding experience that I am forever grateful for.

These two dogs that had a rough start in life have found their happiness in a loving home and with each other. This is rescue. This is the tale of Slim and Sassy.

# Chapter 6

## A Little Roan Dog Named Tucker

Foster name: Tucker

Foster nickname: Little Guy

Foster parent: Susan and Jeff Spaid

Foster state: "Keystone State" – Pennsylvania

Tucker was my first foster. He ended up in my care through a connection with the humane society in Indiana, Pennsylvania. NBRAN had recently done a big rescue with them and since Tucker was a Brittany, my info was passed along to the gentleman that wanted to surrender him. Prior to this, Tucker had gotten loose and was roaming for two weeks in a nature park in Pittsburgh. That is when he met and tangled with a porcupine. Needless to say, the porcupine won. Tucker had an infection and needed medical attention. Tucker's grandpa was scared for him so he talked his son into surrendering him to NBRAN so he could get the care he needed. We met and Tucker was now a part of the NBRAN family. I was so excited when I laid eyes on him because he was a beautiful roan Brittany and I had always wanted one with a roan coat. I knew instantly I wanted to foster him.

When we arrived home, it was immediately evident that my Brittany Scooter did not like Tucker. We had to monitor their interactions closely. My husband took to Tucker right away, and I have a picture I cherish of them laying under a blanket the first night he was home with us. I made a vet appointment so he could be assessed. Tucker had an infection due to impacted quills and my vet was very concerned. She explained to me that the quills imbed in the soft tissue and she would need to open him up to remove them. Tucker was given a strong antibiotic and once the infection was under control, she operated. Thankfully, he came through the surgery well.

Back at home, our Brittany Scooter kept growling and being pushy with Tucker. One day I think Tucker finally had enough. I told my husband it was like Ralphie and Scut Farcus in the movie "A Christmas Story". The character Ralphie finally had enough of Scut's bullying and went after him. This is exactly what Tucker did with Scooter. Thankfully, I was able to grab Tucker before any harm was done but it sure put Scooter in his place. Our boy Scooter looked at him and walked away as if saying "You have earned my respect" in his best Italian

Vito Corleone voice from the movie "The Godfather". After that, the two became best buds.

Once Tucker healed from the porcupine operation, we put him on the adoption website, and a wonderful family in Scranton saw him. The mom was wary because of a previous bad rescue experience she had. The family decided to come and meet Tucker, so they drove three hours with their five year old son for a visit. The young boy played with Tucker, and a short time later he came up and put his little hand on my leg and said, "Susan, when may we have this dog"? I laughed and said, "Well buddy, that's really up to your mom and dad." The mom smiled and said, "We would like to adopt him" so the paperwork was completed and Tucker was theirs. When they were leaving, Tucker jumped in their pickup truck and never looked back. He knew he had found his forever home.

Tucker had a great life with his family. He was able to hunt and walk the nature trails around their home, and he'd go with his dad for coffee every Saturday morning. When he got older the family adopted another dog from NBRAN to help keep Tucker company. After living a full and wonderful life, Tucker passed away. He was his mom's heart dog and she mourned his loss. The family ended up adopting another dog from NBRAN. The son, now a senior in high school, wasn't going to let that dog go anywhere so he lobbied his mom to keep him. This family gave Tucker a wonderful and loving home and continues to open their home to NBRAN dogs. They are a part of our rescue family, all thanks to a little roan dog named Tucker.

## Chapter 7

### MVP Mable

Foster name: Mable

Foster nickname: Mable Bable

Foster parent: Carrie Dezio

Foster state: "Tar Heel State" - North Carolina

Mable was my MVP. She is deemed the most valuable player on my team. This sweet girl joined me as a foster in July of 2019. She was an orange and white Brittany that had the most easygoing, patient, and loving personality. She joined me and my previous foster fail, Bailey. We bonded quickly and soon she was sleeping with Bailey and me every night. Mable grew so attached to me (and I to her) that I knew she would be foster fail number two for me. I just had to keep her.

Mable was pretty sick when she was placed with me. She was approximately 11 years old, and came with a lot of medical needs. To start off, she had a horrible urinary tract infection. After that was resolved, we started her heartworm treatment and she had to go through two rounds of it before she was healed. Anyone who has had to deal with this type of treatment before knows how difficult it can be, but sweet Mable would always bounce back quickly after her treatment injections. She was also dealing with kennel cough and had to go through tooth removal for several bad teeth. Despite all of this, Mable continued to find joy in her daily walks and playing with Bailey. Unfortunately, the hits kept coming when we found a noncancerous tumor on her back. The tumor ruptured and had to be removed. Yet, Mable pressed on. Next, she had to be spayed and went through a mastectomy to remove a lump. As you can see, sweet Mable went through a lot but she continued to impress me with how well she handled everything. I had never met another living creature that continued to find happiness and joy despite all they were going through. She amazed me every day.

One fond memory I have is when I first got Mable. We'd grill fish a lot at home and we'd always give some to Bailey. Fish was new to Mable and when she saw Bailey getting some, it caught her attention. Bailey and Mable gave each other a glance as if saying, "We found the best home because we get yummy seafood here." They were both so happy.

Mable was such a wonderful addition to our pack and family. She passed away unexpectedly in February of this year due to a suspected cancerous mass on her bladder. Bailey and I miss her so much, but I'm grateful she was able to spend the last years of her life being loved by us. The memories of her rolling around on her back and growling with her long legs flailing in the air bring me joy because I know she was happy in her senior years. Mable taught me about patience, and I learned from her that even when we go through trials and tough times, we can still find joy and bounce back. Mable was my MVP and I will always cherish my time with her.

# Chapter 8

## Sweet Dot

Foster name: Dot

Foster nickname: Dottie and Dot-Dot

Foster parent: Cheryl Schuster

Foster state: "The Peach State" - Georgia

I started fostering with NBRAN back in 2010. I had already adopted two Brittanys and decided I would open my home to fostering, too. I had fostered around 10 dogs when Dot came along. She is a beautiful orange and white Brittany with sweet speckles and dots all over that make her coat so special.

When Dot joined our pack, she was a mess. The sadness I saw in her face just broke my heart. Dot had been purchased from a breeder for the purpose of hunting. After approximately five years, she was deemed not hunting material so her owner gave Dot to his daughter. Dot lived outside and was fed with automatic feeders, so she didn't have a lot of physical love or attention from anyone. After three years living this way, she was turned over to NBRAN.

She came to me with a distended belly and with toenails so long they were corkscrewing. She needed a bath and clearly some love and attention. Despite the negligence she had experienced, Dot was a sweet and good natured girl. She knew her name and basic commands, and you could tell she just wanted to be loved.

Since she had lived outdoors without socialization, I wasn't sure how she would adjust indoors, but she has transitioned very well in my home. She gets along great with my other three dogs and enjoys laying on the couch and getting scratches. One of her favorite things to do is to explore the bushes outside where she hunts squirrels and chipmunks. Dot is making up for lost snuggles and love, and she's enjoying the sweet life right now.

One of the things fostering has taught me is to be more empathetic. Fostering has been a healing light in my life over the recent years. I was worried about getting too attached and giving up each dog as I fostered them, but it makes my heart sing when I find a match that will increase both the dog and owner's lives. Fostering has been a real joy for me. I'm so grateful that I've been introduced to this special speckled girl. I'm so thankful for my sweet Dot.

# Chapter 9

## Our Chiefy

Foster name: Chief

Foster nickname: Chiefy

Foster parents: Denise and Ralph Turgeon

Foster state: "The Empire State" - New York

You never forget your first foster because they were the ones who started it all. Here is the story of our first foster named Chief.

We lived in upstate New York at the time when we met him. He was pulled from a shelter and taken into rescue by NBRAN. He was an orange and white male, and we were told he had been an outside dog and would need to learn how to live indoors. After bringing Chief home, we realized that teaching him to be an inside dog was going to be a very easy task. He loved his creature comforts and quickly adapted to our home and routine.

It's hard to describe Chief's personality because it was so very simple and sweet. He was the most laid-back dog we have ever known. He welcomed affection but never came looking for it. He never engaged with other dogs, never played with toys, and never chewed bones. He was quite happy and content in a day which included food, his bed, and the backyard. The only real emotion we'd ever seen from Chief was when it was mealtime or when he thought someone or another dog was in distress. He was like a little old man in a fur coat.

One thing that he loved doing was to explore the backyard and he'd hunt anything that came within reach. Rabbits would sometimes squeeze through the chain link fence and unfortunately for those daring rabbits, Chief's hunting instinct kicked in. There was a time when he even brought one into the house as a prize for me.

In October of 2011, we decided he was here to stay. We adopted him as our first "foster failure". As the years passed, we noticed Chief's cognitive abilities started to decrease. He'd wander around the house and get stuck behind furniture and didn't know how to get out. His hind legs had also weakened to the point where he'd need help getting up. We realized just how serious his condition was when we had left the house for a few hours and returned home to find Chief spread eagle on the floor laying in his urine. He had obviously been in that position for a while, and we were heartbroken to find him like that.

Chief was 14 years old, and the day came when we knew we needed to help ease his pain. We had the vet come to our home for his journey to the Rainbow Bridge where he laid comfortably in his bed surrounded by those that loved him. We would go on to be six more "foster failures" in the future, but we will never forget the one who started it all, our Chiefy.

## Chapter 10

### Sweet to the Very End

Foster name: Sweetie

Foster nickname: Sooie

Foster parents: Larry and Ann Mitchell

Foster state: "The Palmetto State" – South Carolina

Larry and I have had Brittanys for most of our married life. After moving to South Carolina, we thought it would be nice to foster senior and hospice dogs that needed a soft place to land in the last leg of their journey. As odd as that sounds, it was very rewarding for us to show care and love for Brittanys in this stage of their lives.

In August of 2020, I saw this beautiful orange and white senior girl on NBRAN's website, and I just fell in love with her sweet face. She had been owner surrendered by a single mom in Texas who couldn't afford to take care of her. I knew right away that I wanted her to be mine. Her name was Sweetie. She came to us in great health and it was obvious she had been taken care of. She took to our other Brittany and two Boykins right away. She transitioned well into our home and acted as if she had lived here her entire life. Sweetie loved her food and would dance for treats and bark for meals. She liked to go for walks, and she lived up to her namesake by being the sweetest Brittany we've ever had.

We had Sweetie for a few years before she started experiencing neurological issues. She had a mass on her bladder, and in March of 2022, we lovingly helped her cross the Rainbow Bridge. It broke our hearts but she was at peace.

It's very rewarding to be a foster and adopter of these rescue dogs. There is a saying in fostering that says "your heart breaks a little so theirs never has to break again," and this is so true. I always shed tears when they leave because I will miss them, but I find joy in seeing them move on to new owners who will love them. We are grateful for each foster that has come through our home and Sweetie is no exception. We are so thankful for the time we had with her in the last chapter of her life. Sweetie showed us exactly why we love the seniors because she was sweet to the very end.

# Chapter 11

## Buster

Foster name: Buster

Foster nickname: Bud

Foster parents: Denise and Ralph Turgeon

Foster state: "The Sunshine State" – Florida

It would be unfair to talk about the foster experience without talking about the hard and heartbreaking ones. I want to share Buster's story with you all because he deserves his story to be heard.

About two years ago, we fostered a two year old orange and white male whose owner had passed away. He was given to people who didn't want him. They kept him tied outside 24 hours a day, and a concerned neighbor convinced the family to surrender him to rescue. His name was Buster.

He was brought to a vet clinic in Mississippi for boarding and evaluation until he could be transported to us in Florida to foster him. An NBRAN volunteer went to visit him the day before transport, and while she was petting him, Buster bit her hand. It was easy to assume that he was just nervous being in an unfamiliar environment, but little did we know, that was just the beginning.

Buster arrived in Florida after his long transport. He was full of energy and just wanted to run around the yard. We began slow introductions with our Brittany girls but within seconds, Buster had lunged for one of them causing a wound to her forehead. Thankfully, he was on a leash and was quickly brought under control. At that point, we knew we had to keep him away from the other dogs until we were confident he would settle down. Unfortunately, that never came to be.

We had to section off the house with baby gates to keep them separated, and Buster's aggressive behavior was evident every time the girls got near. He'd growl and snarl viciously to let them know to stay away. As NBRAN fosters, we work with all personality types and behavioral issues. Some of these dogs have had rough lives and it's important to help them in any way we can. Buster was no different.

We contacted a behaviorist to get help on how to manage his aggressive behavior. We didn't know what all he'd been through, but it was obvious something was triggering him. We followed the training we received, but nothing seemed to work. There were three separate occasions when my husband would go and sit next to Buster and without warning, he was met with teeth and a bite. Buster would latch on to his hand and not let go. It became clear to us that something was very wrong. Buster would not be adoptable. The liability was too great and for the safety of others, we couldn't pass him on to someone else. In situations like this we also want to do what's best for the dog. After discussing the situation with NBRAN, the decision was made to euthanize Buster. It was a heart-wrenching decision because he was a young, beautiful male who had a long life ahead of him if not for his aggressive behavior.

A vet appointment was made to have him euthanized. We wanted to be with him so that he wasn't scared, and so he knew he was loved. As I sat on the floor next to him, Buster clamped down on my hand and would not let go. My husband had to pry his jaw open but not after inflicting enough damage to warrant a trip to the emergency room for my hand.

Buster's life came to a tragic end in a way that cannot be explained. We never knew or could determine what his triggers were. I spoke to the vet afterward and asked if he had ever seen behavior like this before. He admitted that he had not and said Buster was most likely "not wired right." If we were to name a foster dog who has changed us the most, it would be Buster. Not knowing what was wrong with him or how to fix him made us feel helpless and emotionally drained. It seemed like a complete waste for what should have been a wonderful life for a beautiful, young dog. We are more cautious about approaching dogs we don't know now. Our experience with Buster, although heart-wrenching and difficult, reminds us that we don't know what these dogs have gone through in their past, and it opens our hearts even more to show love to those that cross our paths. Even though this foster story had a sad ending, we wanted to honor Buster's story by sharing it. We will always remember him.

# Chapter 12

## Maddie's Chair

Foster name: Maddie

Foster nickname: Miss Maddie

Foster parent: Leslie and Paul Demmert

Foster state: "Keystone State" – Pennsylvania

We foster because we can. Others adopt and many work in shelters or in rescue. These are the frontline workers for dogs. They are safety nets for the ones that have lost their homes and need to find new ones. We have been fortunate enough to foster many and adopt some along the way.

One of our fosters was Maddie. She was an orange and white Brittany that was found on New Year's Day swimming in a creek with a stick wedged in between her gums. Her chip was outdated and when her humans were eventually found, they didn't want her back. She was held in a shelter until she was rescued by NBRAN.

When we picked her up, she jumped right onto my husband's lap and stayed there for nearly two hours while we drove home. She must've been loved at one time because her manners were impeccable. Once we arrived home, we introduced her to the pack and everyone got along well. In her first day at our house she managed to pick out a few of her favorite toys (all the ones with squeakers) and ended the evening cuddling with our grouchy eight year old Brittany named Kilo. She had officially been accepted into the pack.

Maddie had many health issues that we had to work through. She had been infested with fleas when she was plucked out of the creek, and she had a horrible yeast infection in both ears. She was between five and eight years old and had a tapeworm that was being addressed. She also had some skin issues that were being managed with proper medications. Maddie had a corneal scratch, a cataract, and would soon undergo spay surgery along with the removal of a walnut sized mammary tumor. Although she had many health issues, we were addressing them all and she was showing improvement.

Maddie continued to settle in nicely at our house and even had a favorite chair. She was the first foster to see me as anything other than the maid who doles out kibble. Even our independent eight year old named Gambol has allowed her to share his bed. Maddie is 10-15 pounds lighter than our three male dogs, but she has put the message out that she's the big girl on the block. Her actions show that she is self-assured; she takes bones, toys, and even sticks her head in the other dog's bowls and our boys just stand back and let her do it. She has made herself right at home.

One fun routine we have at our house is our after-dinner "tricks for treats" game. This is when I take them through their routine of sit, down, shake, paw, and roll over. My boys are very familiar with this nightly routine but it's new to Maddie and I was surprised to see how many tricks she knew. She is very food motivated and caught on by watching the other dogs and after months of training, I could place a treat on her nose and she could snatch it out of the air on the "okay" command. Maddie was simply a dream lady, and we loved having her around.

Our foster time with Maddie came to an end when she was adopted. We really do our homework to make sure that we find the best homes and fit for each dog. Maddie's potential family enjoyed RV-camping and wanted a dog who was social and that loved people. That fit Maddie perfectly. They lived about 75 minutes from us so they took a drive one afternoon to meet Maddie in her environment. We invited the prospective mom to sit in what we now called "Maddie's chair" and within seconds Maddie was in her lap and the adoption was complete. Maddie is such a loving dog and, although it was hard to see her go, we knew she'd have a great life. Maddie and her new family have been to visit us several times, and when she comes into the house she jumps right back into her chair as if she'd never left.

# Chapter 13

## Perfect Max

Foster name: Max

Foster nickname: Maximus Dogious

Foster parent: Dave, Mary, Michael, and Thomas Voeltz

Foster state: "The Mount Rushmore State" - South Dakota

We had fostered many dogs by the time we met Max in March of 2003. He was a smaller white and tan male that was surrendered by his owner and dropped at a shelter. It was a mystery to us as to why he was there because Max was the perfect dog. We picked him up at the Rapid City, S.D., Humane Society and he immediately settled in for the three-hour car ride home. As custom for all new dogs, Max was led around to the fenced-in backyard to do his business and sniff the telltale evidence of the other dogs that had been there. After he stretched his legs, my wife let our dogs out, one at a time, to introduce them to our new houseguest. He stood there with his tail stub wiggling and allowed the other dogs to sniff him and never complained once. He almost acted like a puppy the way he played, and only the grey on his muzzle revealed his true age.

He was house-trained and had the best manners. He'd sit patiently and wait to be fed, and he'd willingly go in to his kennel. When we allowed him to roam free in the house, he never damaged anything. He wasn't high energy and was content taking it easy and chilling with his people. One of his favorite things to do was to place his head in your lap. He was respectful to other dogs, very gentle with children, and was in heaven when he could go for a car ride. Max was the perfect dog.

Once home, I took him to the vet to get his shots and check his overall health. My vet discovered a lump on his neck and suggested a biopsy. We soon discovered that Max had thyroid cancer. Further exams and x-rays determined that treatment options were limited. While we could put him through painful treatment, it wasn't going to extend his life. We made the decision to bring Max home. Our plan was to spoil him rotten, love him as much as we could, and make his final weeks the best of his life. My vet estimated he had about four months to live. If he made it to the 4th of July, it would be a call for celebration but, once again, he would astonish us in more ways than one.

To the casual observer you'd never know Max was sick. He was always happy and a joy to be around. One day I came home from work, stretched out my arms and cried "MAXIMUS" in a loud voice and to my amazement, Max stood up and walked towards me on his hind legs and embraced me with a big hug. I was absolutely shocked. My wife could not believe her eyes. I picked him up and gave him a long loving embrace. It was incredible.

We took Max camping in the spring, and he loved it. He would stand facing the wind with his ears blowing in the breeze. He'd sniff the air and simply enjoyed life. He was fond of bird watching and kept a close eye on the squirrels running about. Besides his love for the outdoors, he equally loved getting his head rubbed. He'd contently sit back in lawn chairs and watch the campfire while we roasted marshmallows. To him, this was paradise.

Spring turned to summer and Max was doing great. He showed absolutely no indication of affliction, but the telltale swelling of his neck was a constant reminder of the demon within. The Fourth of July arrived and Max was still going strong. He had lived longer than expected and every day from this point was a bonus. We were now praying that he would make it to Labor Day. To our surprise, Max lived to see Labor Day, Halloween, Thanksgiving, Christmas,

Valentine's Day, another spring, and even Easter. We were hoping that he was going to live forever.

Max had one tree that he loved to urinate on each time he took care of business. While I encouraged him to go elsewhere, he was going to mark that tree as his very own. While he did manage to clear the grass growth about a foot around the perimeter, I didn't mind. We affectionately named it "Max's Tree" and it stands today as a tribute to the "loving care" he showered on it.

Max had unique feathering on his rear legs. It almost looked like he was wearing baggy pants. Each morning as we got up we would tell him to put his pants on. He probably wondered what these silly humans were talking about. As April ended, we noticed that Max was starting to walk stiff legged. He didn't show any signs of pain, but when our vet checked him, she was afraid the cancer was invading his nervous system and his time was drawing near. We carried him up and down the steps, and he was still determined to "water" his tree.

About a week and a half later, Max was resting on the couch as we were watching television. Suddenly, his body tensed up and he was stiff as a board. It was as if he were a statue. Other than being able to blink his eyes and move his mouth, all of his other functions were frozen. I slept on the floor with him that night trying to comfort him. On the morning of May 10, 2004, we made the final visit to the vet. We speculate the cancer entered his nervous system and short circuited it. I held Max's stiff body on my lap and gently caressed his head as he received the final relief medication. He looked up at me with his loving eyes and as they slowly closed, his frozen body relaxed and he was at peace.

Max's death shook me to my core. I seriously contemplated giving up fostering. I didn't think I could have my heart broken like that again, but then I started thinking about the other Maxes out there waiting for someone special to come along. I knew I needed to go on. We have continued fostering over the years and have seen many dogs come and go. Max was the second foster dog that crossed the Rainbow Bridge while in our care. Thankfully, we haven't had any heartbreaks as bad as we did with him. I will never forget our perfect boy Max.

## Chapter 14

### Half-Brother Surprise

Foster name: Pinot

Foster nickname: Mr. Long Feathers

Foster parent: Sara Mehle

Foster state: "The Old Dominion" – Virginia

One day in 2018, I was walking my Brittany Moose in a lively neighborhood in Richmond, Virginia, when a lady stopped me. She complimented Moose and told me that her co-worker did a lot of work with NBRAN. I had never heard of this rescue before but something urged me to get involved. I had a deep love for this breed because we had many Brittanys growing up (Betsy, Louis, Esther, and Joey). My parents currently have a pack of three (Lilly, Wilson, and Clifford) so Brittanys are in my blood.

I reached out to NBRAN right away and was able to connect with the Virginia coordinator, Leslie Trenta. I knew that being in a one-bedroom loft apartment with a 14-year-old rescue cat and a nine-month-old Brittany might be a turn off for NBRAN, but I was determined to help out wherever I could. The first NBRAN volunteer I interacted with was a woman named Sheila who holds a special place in my heart along with her Brittany Penny. Shelia came over for my home walk-through and approved me for volunteering. Not too long after that, I took my first ride on the Brittany railroad to help with transporting Brittanys.

One day just before we celebrated Moose's first birthday, I was asked to help with an owner surrender in the Richmond area. I jumped at the opportunity. I drove to rescue my first Brittany. His name was Pinot and he was a beautiful orange and white two-year-old that was being owner surrendered. I looked at his papers and noticed right away that my Brittany Moose and Pinot had the same dad. They were half-brothers. I couldn't think of a better gift for Moose than meeting his sibling that day. It was so special.

We took Pinot home where he instantly made himself comfortable by jumping all the way up on the kitchen counter with all four paws. Andre the cat was not thrilled, but we found a way to make it work. Moose was so loving towards our new houseguest and he took to his half-brother immediately. It was as if they knew they were family. When I had to go to work I'd watch Moose and

Pinot on the pet camera snuggling together throughout the day. They'd play together and cuddle at night and it was precious to see their immediate bond.

It didn't take long for Pinot to be adopted so our time with him was short. Pinot moved on to his forever home in Florida with another dog named Pepper. He's had trips to visit Santa and gets lot of snuggles from his new family. Since then, I have continued to foster and volunteer with NBRAN. I have made many lifelong friends and am so grateful for my experience with them. I'm excited to continue serving alongside this great organization with Moose by my side.

## Chapter 15

### Never Say Never

Foster name: Jack

Foster nickname: Jack Jack

Foster parent: Jenny and Mark Kostlan

Foster state: "Tar Heel State" – North Carolina

Our story started after we lost our amazing dog Duke. Duke embodied all of the qualities of the perfect dog. After losing him, our other dog Mitzi lost a part of herself. Not only did we lose our best friend but so did she. Duke was the comfort in the chaos for Mitzi, and she was lost without him. We all were.

My sister is a coordinator for NBRAN so I talked with her about finding Mitzi a companion, and she recommended fostering. My husband Mark and I talked it over and we decided we'd give fostering a try. We built a fence to make sure the new dog(s) would be safe and our foster journey began.

We've had many fosters along the way. Some, like Bullet, were crazy and had us doubting if fostering was right for us. Yet others, like Tubbs, Ruger, Cooper 1, Cooper 2, and sweet Lilly, would come along and make it all worth it. We were enjoying our time in this new foster parent role, and it was very rewarding. These dogs became family to us, and we have a special routine of giving each one their own engraved name tag and harness. We took on the mentality that they were ours until it was time for them to go to their forever homes, and it was fulfilling and special for us to be a part of this.

My husband had always said, "We can foster Brittanys but we will never adopt one." Like the saying goes "never say never" because along came Jack. We had another rescue dog named Rex at the time as well. Jack had been found wandering on someone's property, and he needed a foster home. When I picked him up I was greeted by this beautiful liver and white boy. He immediately bonded with our kids and both Rex and Mitzi when he arrived. Jack was a total goofball. His motto in life is "if it flies, it dies." He chases everything from birds, bees, moths, lizards, rabbits, and mice. When we first brought him home he didn't give anyone kisses. I don't think he knew what they were. He was fearful; almost like you could see the abuse from the past. But now, he gives the best smooches ever, and he loves to snuggle. He fit right in with our pack.

Just as quick as Jack arrived home with us, tragedy struck when Rex passed away unexpectedly from a congenital heart defect. Our family was heartbroken and Jack stepped in to comfort us all. Jack was exactly what we needed at just the right time. He'd follow my husband around, and he was so gentle and loving towards us. One night I was talking to Mark and he said, "What if we foster failed Jack and adopted him?" I was shocked because this was the man that said "never will we ever." I was so excited. The next morning our kids asked us if we could keep Jack and with glances towards each other, we both said yes. It was the best decision we've ever made for our family. We never imagined we'd foster fail. It wasn't in the plan. But Jack was. He fit right in. He was the plug to the gaping hole that we had felt since losing Duke and now Rex. Jack is perfect for us. He has become our protector, and he loves us with his whole heart. He is teaching our other dog, Willow, how to behave and Mitzi watches from the side, as an almost 15-year-old dog now. She approves of Jack and is ready to pass the torch to him with welcoming new fosters into our lives. If there is one thing besides true love that Jack has taught us it's to never say never. We are forever grateful for our beloved Jack.

# Chapter 16

## Bernie's Journey

Foster name: Bernie

Foster nickname: Bun Bun and Bunny

Foster parents: Roberta and Bill Ruck

Foster state: "The Buckeye State" - Ohio

My foster story with Bernie began in July of 2013. We had just lost our Springer Meg to a mast cell tumor and we were heartbroken. I saw that a five-year-old boy named Bernie needed a foster so we volunteered. Bernie was a stray living in the woods of West Virginia. A persistent good Samaritan thinks he'd been living there for over a year. He was finally able to catch him and contacted NBRAN. I picked him up and quickly realized the poor shape he was in. He was covered in demodectic mange. Bernie's back leg was atrophied and painful for him to put down. After seeing the vet it was determined that Bernie had been shot in the ankle causing serious injury. We were trying to figure out if he'd need a leg amputation when we heard news that a vet in Cincinnati could save his leg. It was a blessing because the surgeon had an opening for the very next day. Bernie underwent surgery to repair his shattered ankle so he could have use of his leg again.

When I picked Bernie up he looked like a little Brittany Frankenstein. He had staples, a patch for his epidural, and a cast all the way up his leg. He would need to be in that cast for 18 weeks for his ankle and leg to heal properly. Bernie was such a great patient and healed very well. After his cast came off and with physical therapy, Bernie had full use of his leg. With everything we'd been through with Bernie, I just couldn't see giving him up. In March of 2014, I gave my husband Bernie's adoption paperwork as an anniversary present and he was ours.

I remember taking Bernie to Malabar Farms for our bi-annual NBRAN get-together where he got to meet his rescuers, and he was always the NBRAN ambassador when we'd go to dog shows or pet events. Just over a year later, the pin in Bernie's leg started to come out so he needed surgery again and was in a cast for another 18 weeks. He always took it in stride and never complained. It was as if he knew he was being cared for and knew he needed to heal. After this surgery it was hard for him to bend his leg, so we started water therapy once a week so he could strengthen it.

While all of this was happening, we had fostered two more Brittanys that we ended up adopting so we had five Brittanys in the house. Bernie was always the annoying little brother who was mostly tolerated. Although he didn't really play with toys, he'd steal them and take them up to his lair in our bedroom closet and hide them. He never knew he had a bum leg and loved to chase cars down the fence line. After all that time in the woods he'd still sleep like a bird with his head under his leg and eat berries right off the bush. Bernie was a survivor after all.

At 14.5 years old, Bernie had outlived all of his other Britt siblings. He still enjoyed the simple things in life like going for short walks and sitting out on the patio with the wind blowing through his long silvered ears. Just before his 15th birthday, Bernie started having kidney failure. His leg was giving him issues and it was suspected that he had cancer. He led a triumphant life and it was time to give him peace so we helped him cross the Rainbow Bridge. Bernie had so much strength and kindness in his soul, and he impacted our lives in ways we couldn't imagine. His legacy carries on through us, and we are so grateful for Bernie and his courageous journey.

# Chapter 17

## Bear's Purpose

Foster name: Bear

Foster nickname: Big Bear

Foster parent: Dave, Mary, Michael, and Thomas Voeltz

Foster state: "The Mount Rushmore State" – South Dakota

Fostering can be very rewarding, but it is not without some truly painful experiences as well. Let me introduce you to a brown and white Brittany named Bear. He was a big wooly boy with a heart of gold. He was a fun-loving dog and, other than liking to dig under the fence, was a perfect houseguest. Bear came to foster with us and things were going well. He got along great with my older son, Michael and we were glad to have him with us.

After fostering him for a few weeks, we determined that his medical issue was having seizures. Looking at the big picture, this was a treatable and manageable ailment, so we started medication. Bear was starting to get comfortable with us, and we were getting comfortable with him. He was house trained and earned the privilege of not being kenneled while home alone. He made himself comfortable at the end of our sectional couch, played well with our other dogs, and settled nicely into our pack.

His downfall, as we would learn, was his love to destroy and eat braded chew ropes. He'd spend all day tossing them in the air, pouncing on them, and ripping them apart. I thought this was a good activity for him and it entertained him for hours. Little did I know what was really happening; Bear was eating the thread as he pulled the ropes apart. After three weeks, Bear was not able to keep food or water down. We knew something was wrong. My vet took x-rays, and an obstruction was found in his intestines. The only cure was an expensive emergency operation. Of course, NBRAN didn't hesitate to approve it and Bear underwent successful surgery. Our vet warned us there could be complications, and it would be a 50/50 chance of a full recovery. It appeared he beat the odds and was recovering well. In an instant, everything changed. Bear collapsed while resting in his kennel at the vet and, in spite of her best efforts, she was not able to revive him. We weren't sure of the exact cause of his passing but suspect it was from a blood clot that formed and broke loose from his surgery.

His loss hit us hard. This was the first time that a foster dog crossed over the Rainbow Bridge while under our care. I was devastated and felt like I let Bear and NBRAN down. We did almost everything right and still failed him. There was a place north of town that served as a pet cemetery. My family purchased a plot and Bear was laid to rest. We lovingly wrapped him in his blanket and the owners of the land gently placed him in the earth. Now over 20 years later, the trees have grown tall and his grave sits in the shade of one of the many trees that protect him and the other beloved pets resting there.

We decided to take a break for a few months from fostering. This was our first failure, and I wasn't sure if I was worthy to be entrusted in the care of another dog. Even though we did everything we could, I felt so guilty about Bear's passing. As my heart and soul recovered, I knew I had to give this horrible experience a purpose. I did not want Bear to die in vain. I threw out all of the chew ropes and shared with everyone I knew about the dangers of them. I also went on a popular national radio talk show and shared the dangers of those kinds of toys. I was hoping to save as many dogs as I could from this horrible death. I became good friends with Bruce, the talk show host, and in the years to come we'd have many conversations about our dogs together. When his Boston Terrier Mickie died, I shared my version of the Dog's Prayer with him. He also read this prayer on air the day before our beloved Molly crossed the Rainbow Bridge. Bear's passing did result in a new friendship and advocate for animal welfare, so there was some good from it. However, to this very day, I still have terrible guilt. Bear has a purpose, and it's to save other dog's lives. Although it came at a great cost, his legacy continues on, and more dogs are being saved.

# Chapter 18

## Daddy's Girl

Foster name: Molly

Foster nickname: Molly Sue

Foster parents: David and Brenda Pantleo

Foster state: "The Show-Me State" - Missouri

In June of this year my wife and I will be married 43 years. We've always had at least one Brittany in our lives. In fact, before we were married I had been around this breed all my life. My grandfather started the Missouri Brittany Club years ago. I would go to field trials and dog shows all the time. Growing up I was surrounded by Brittanys because my parents owned and raised them and I always loved this breed because of their willingness and desire to be your faithful companion. At this time in our lives, we had an energetic three-year-old Brittany named Macie. We purchased her through a reputable breeder to be used as a diabetic alert dog. Because of her energy level, we thought it best to adopt another dog that could be a playmate to exhaust some of that high energy that Britts are known for.

Since we wanted a rescue, we joined and started following several different Brittany groups on social media. After researching NBRAN, we joined their fostering program. As of March 2022, we've had nine fosters come through our home. If it was my wife's choice, we would've adopted them all. At times it can be very difficult to let them go but, if we'd kept them all we wouldn't be able to help the next dog. We always said our tearful goodbyes so we could welcome the next foster into our home. That is how we did things until Molly came along.

Molly is an orange and white roan 11 year old that came to us with a heartbreaking past. She'd been disciplined with a heavy hand and developed bad anxiety from her previous owner. She came to us with difficult health issues too. As soon as she arrived we met with a cardiologist who diagnosed her with a grade five heart murmur. Due to everything she had been through, Molly was a timid and scared little girl.

When she was home with us it was obvious that she found comfort and safety being near me. To say she is my Velcro dog is an understatement. Molly follows me everywhere. If I go to my office to work, Molly is there. When I come home, Molly's there waiting for me. When I leave a room, Molly goes too. We even have baby gates up around the house to keep the dogs out of certain rooms, and Molly has figured out how to open each gate so she can be by my side. There are times I take our other dog for a walk, and Molly just stares out the door whining until I get home. Due to her heart condition, we have to be careful how much energy she exhausts, but she's always ready to go on short walks around the block with me. She doesn't walk fast and is usually a step or two behind. When I look over my shoulder to check on her, she looks up at me as if saying, "Am I doing ok daddy?" I always respond with "good girl, Molly" and I swear she joyfully smiles back. When we get home, she gets a drink and comes and sits by me or my wife for her afternoon siesta.

One day I told my wife I was taking Molly for a car ride. I opened the door, we went out to the garage, and Molly stood politely waiting for me. I opened the car door, and she stood up on the floor board waiting for me to lift her in the car like it was a daddy/daughter date. Once inside she laid down, and we drove around the block for a short drive. When we got home, she acted as if we had just gotten back from a long journey together. She didn't care how far we went; just that she got to go. We have the same routine when it's bed time. Molly walks into the bedroom and waits for me to pick her up so she can find her special spot on the bed and settle down for the night.

Molly's medical issues, such as heart murmur, arrhythmia, mammary tumor, and horrible dental issues, have been taken care of. She's responding well to medication, and we are hopeful she will be able to live out the rest of her days and years happily. She has settled into a nice routine in our home with our pack and is learning all the basic commands. If she needs to go out, she has learned to ring the bell. If there is one thing I can say about this daddy's girl it's that she loves to be with her people. Since being with us, we've seen her blossom and grow in so many ways. To say Molly has stolen a piece of our heart is an understatement. She has impacted us so much by her loving and caring nature. Molly has recently been made a hospice dog, and we felt it best for her that she stay right here living with us. Daddy's girl can now stay and live the life she was always meant to live being loved by us. There will be other fosters come and go, but none like our Molly girl.

# Chapter 19

## 1,279 Days

Foster name: Gracie

Foster nickname: Gracers

Foster parents: Laura and Collin Ryerson

Foster state: "The Golden State" – California

One thousand, two hundred, and seventy-nine days. That is how long we were able to love our sweet Gracie girl. She came into our lives on November 4, 2017, at approximately nine years old. Gracie had been left at an animal shelter along with two other dogs. NBRAN became aware of her, and when they went to get her she was scared, shutdown, and curled up in a ball. Thankfully, her story didn't end there. It was a new day for sweet Gracie; day one.

When she arrived home my husband knew that very moment that she wasn't going anywhere. We instantly fell in love with her sweet and gentle spirit. Gracie had some health issues and underwent a few surgeries to remove mammary tumors and be spayed. Thankfully she healed well and quickly became my Velcro dog, never leaving my side. She fit in perfectly with our family and was immensely loved by us and our one-and-a-half-year old daughter, Sienna. We also had a male Brittany named Cooper and both he and Gracie adjusted well to each other. As the days passed, their bond grew strong. So did ours. Gracie was doing well and adjusting to the good life at home with us in El Dorado Hills.

As the days continued to tick by, Gracie found her stride and settled in nicely. She enjoyed daily adventures like squirrel hunting in the parks, running at the dog park, and exploring trails. Both dogs spent weekends with us in South Lake Tahoe hiking, playing in the creeks, and enjoying beach days. In looking back at the hundreds of photos and videos we took of her, I find peace in knowing there was never a dull moment in her final years. She was either outside with us walking, hiking, and playing, or she was inside cozy on the couch receiving non-stop love and pets from all of us. I worked from home so she was never alone, and when Gracie met new people they'd always comment on how cute and sweet she was. She'd often steal the show from our handsome boy Cooper and people usually couldn't even tell that she was a senior girl.

One of my favorite memories I have is the pure happiness I felt watching her blissfully run through the tall Tahoe meadow grass taking in all the smells. You could almost see a joyful smile come across her face. She'd make funny little noises when she was being petted and had a soft snore while sleeping. Gracie also had a beautiful howl when she barked that made our hearts soar. As most dogs are, she was a lover of cheese and would not leave the kitchen while we cooked. She truly loved our daughter, Sienna, and loved resting her head on her daddy's leg. She especially loved it when I would rub her sweet ears.

As days and years passed, we noticed that she started experiencing cognitive dysfunction. I loved her even more as I lifted, held, and carried her more often than not, trying to figure out how to keep her comfortable with the simple aspects of life. She was getting very disoriented at home and eventually even struggled with eating and drinking. We still took walks in her favorite park, and I did everything I could to help her get as much hydration as she could manage. It was a very intense and challenging time, but we were trying to do everything we could for our Gracie girl while keeping her quality of life in mind. She started to grow distant, but I knew that she still recognized me, and I gave her everything I had until her condition became too much for her.

We loved our Gracie girl for 1,279 days. For nearly four years, she gave us unconditional love and we gave it right back. She entered our world on day one and left it physically on May 6, 2021, surrounded by our family as she laid in my arms while we helped her cross the Rainbow Bridge. We loved her with all our hearts. We are thankful for the memories, pictures, and videos we have of her. We are grateful for 1,279 days.

# Chapter 20

## Ellie's Story

Foster name: Ellie

Foster nickname: Ellie Bird, Ellie Mae, Boykin, Bird Dog

Foster parent: Dave, Mary, Michael, and Thomas Voeltz

Foster state: "The Mount Rushmore State" – South Dakota

We first learned of Ellie in November 2012 from a fellow rescuer in Minnesota. She saw her in a Cannon Falls Shelter when checking on another dog for her rescue, and she contacted me. Based on her picture, Ellie looked like a French Brittany or possibly a Boykin. Either way, I agreed to immediately take her in as a foster. We wanted to get her out of the shelter right away so a temporary foster home was found while we worked on the arrangements to get her transported to our home in Pierre. Thankfully, the temporary foster agreed to care for Ellie for three weeks until she could be transported home to us. Finally on December 22, Ellie was on her way to Pierre. We anxiously awaited her arrival. Once she was dropped off, we immediately noticed the pictures we had seen of her did not do her justice. She has a brown coat with speckles of black and white, and she was absolutely beautiful.

We went through the normal introduction process we use when introducing new dogs into the pack. Things went fairly well, although Ellie was a bit dominant and authoritative towards the other dogs. It was obvious she favored people over canines, so we knew we'd need to work on that. Another thing we noticed was that Ellie had a slight limp on her rear leg. We took her in to the vet to have it x-rayed where we discovered a metal rod in her leg from a previous injury. Someone had spent a large sum of money repairing this leg, and I couldn't imagine they would have abandoned her after making this kind of investment. We were going to make every effort to try to find her owners. Over the next two months, I checked in with all of the shelters in a 75-mile radius to see if they knew of anyone looking. Law enforcement was contacted to see if any of them had reports of a lost dog. We saturated social media in an attempt to find her owner, but everything we did was a dead end. While we didn't give up, we were not optimistic that her owner would be found.

While this was happening, Ellie was making herself at home and spent every second by our side. She loved sitting on our lap and sleeping at our side at night. She was adjusting to the other foster dogs in the house and was transitioning well. Ellie was working her way into our hearts. Finally, after three months of trying to locate her owner, a decision was made to put her up for adoption. We bonded with her so quickly and didn't want to see her go so we put in an application to adopt her and on March 19, 2013, she was officially ours.

Over time, Ellie has learned to be less bossy and to be more tolerant of other dogs. With the parade of foster dogs that have passed through our home, she has learned to help them adapt to being houseguests. She has been instrumental in helping us get them house trained as well. I would take her and the new foster out and give the command "go potty" and Ellie would do her business. The foster dogs would see this and understood what was expected. Of course it is always funny to watch Ellie as she closely monitors them and then quickly runs over to mark on their scent. That must be the dominance left in her. Overall, she has been a great teacher to our foster dogs over the years.

It's been nine years and Ellie is still here with us. Her muzzle is graying, cataracts are developing in her eyes, and she can't jump as high as she could when she was younger. She's still a loving dog that enjoys the simple things in life like looking for squirrels in the park and the occasional treat. She loves going camping and spending hours relaxing in the sun during the day and begging for s'mores around the campfire at night. We give her a small bite of graham cracker and she is happy for about a minute, and then she starts begging all over again. Something she is fond of is going for car rides and riding shotgun on outbound foster transports. She loves riding in the car whether it's a long ride to Rapid City or a short ride to church. This summer we are trying something new. My wife and I like riding our motorcycle around town and I built a secure trailer to pull behind the cycle so Ellie and our other dog, Olive, can ride inside. While I would never take them out on the highway, I think they will enjoy the leisurely rides around town. We are looking forward to trying it out once the weather gets nice.

Ellie is still quite vocal and squeals like a stuck hog when she hears us come home. She jumps for joy, runs in circles, and cries like she hasn't seen us for a year. While some might find this annoying, we don't mind a bit. Ellie has been a complete joy, and we are blessed to have had her come into our lives and pray that the Great Master allows her to stick around for a few more years so we can share her love.

# Chapter 21

## Bandit the Heart Stealer

Foster name: Bandit

Foster nickname: Bandito

Foster parents: Lisa and Jeff Blystone

Foster state: "KeyStone State" - Pennsylvania

We are Lisa and Jeff Blystone and we live in Marysville, Pennsylvania. Between us we have six adult kids, and we've always had dogs in our home. We moved to Marysville in 2015 and purchased 10 acres of land with a one-acre fenced in yard that was perfect for our pack. Over the years we've expanded our animal population from dogs to 14 chickens and now three goats. As you can see, we are a family of animal lovers.

We fell into fostering for NBRAN on New Year's Eve in 2017. A good friend of ours saw a man who was trying to sell an eight-month-old liver and white Brittany on Facebook. She was able to get him to surrender the dog to NBRAN, and that is when his new life began. His name is Bandit and he would soon steal our hearts. We found out quickly that Bandit had been crated for most of his young life. He needed to learn manners, basic commands, and we needed to learn the best way to introduce him to our big family and pack of four. We determined introducing them one at a time would work out best. With each dog's personality came a different reaction to the new member of the house. After a few hours and lots of sniffing tails, everyone calmed down and the house was now a peaceful pack of five.

Bandit had a lot to learn, and so did we. He needed to learn how to be a dog, and we needed to learn how to be foster parents. One decision we made was to take him everywhere with us. Bandit went with us to Lowes, Home Depot, Tractor Supply, and anywhere else dogs were allowed to go. Bandit did great running errands, and his personality was really starting to blossom. He is a very sweet boy that loves to cuddle. He is easy-going and, like our 14 chickens, he's an early riser. Since he had been crated for so long, he quickly learned the freedom and joy that came with our fenced in yard. His little feet were like the legs of a Road Runner; just a constant blur as he ran around stretching his legs. He'd chase shadows and learned how important treats were for a growing puppy. He was learning all the basic commands and most importantly, Bandit was learning how to be loved. He was flourishing in his new life, and we were too.

After two months, Bandit was put up for adoption and a family in New Jersey was interested in him. This was very bittersweet for our family because we all loved him. There were times we thought he'd stay living with us forever, but we'd been bitten by the "foster bug" and knew we wanted to continue to rescue and foster other dogs. Our family farm was already bursting at the seams, and if we'd kept him we wouldn't be able to help the next Brittany in need. With that, we met Bandits new parents. We said our tearful goodbyes as he headed for the coast to live with his forever family and new Brittany brother named Sparky.

Bandit will always hold a special place in our heart because he introduced us to NBRAN and was our first foster. He reinforced our love of animals and encouraged us to continue to foster more dogs. Fostering has been very rewarding for us because we're helping a Brittany get ready for their new "fur-ever" home. We share the greatest love with these dogs and provide them a new life, a new home, and a new family. Happy tears have been shed as we hand over the leash to new parents, and we've been fortunate to keep in touch with adoptive families. We are blessed in knowing that we play a part in helping these beautiful Brittanys live the lives they are meant to live; happy, joyful, and loved.

There will continue to be more fosters that grace our homestead, and they will continue to come and go, but we will always hold a special place in our heart for our first foster, the heart stealer Bandit.

## Chapter 22

### Brave Brady

Foster name: Brady

Foster nickname: Porky

Foster parents: Leslie and Paul Demmert

Foster state: "Keystone State" - Pennsylvania

We had always been foster parents to senior dogs, and that is what we knew. This all changed when Brady came along. Brady was approximately one to two years old and has strong orange markings on his coat. He had been rescued from a farm that had no electricity or running water. The rescuer said the outside was cleaner than the inside of the house. Brady had a Brittany sibling with him and they were both very stinky dogs. It was clear they had not received any kind of medical attention in their young lives. They were intact, had full Brittany tails along with dewclaws. Surprisingly they were heartworm negative and were not tick or flea infested. They were small and thin but didn't appear malnourished. Brady's sibling went to another foster out East and Brady came home to foster with us.

We quickly realized that Brady was blind in both eyes. We thought he may need a seeing-eye helper, but it appears he can see light and he manages pretty well on his own. Due to being confined to a crate for most of his young life, he looks as if he may have muscle atrophy in his legs. Even just walking 100 yards tires him out quickly. Although he had suffered such terrible living conditions, he was remarkably brave. When we first picked him up from his rescuer, he went flat belly down. He tried to slide away and didn't want anything to do with people and he had to be carried to our car. It took the entire two-hour car ride home snuggling next to my husband Paul for him to realize he was safe. Brady was coming out of his shell and becoming brave.

Once we got him home, he'd rest on the hard but cool tile floor, although there were comfy beds, pillows and rugs nearby. He'd drink an entire bowl of water at one time because he probably learned from his previous owner to drink every last drop because there was no telling when more would be available. It was clear to us that Brady simply needed to learn how to be a loved dog. He went to the vet the day after he arrived for a full work up. He was given shots, a mouth and eye exam, and the vet attended to a few open sores on his legs. His front teeth were worn down to nubs from probably chewing on his environment to alleviate boredom. Over the next few weeks, we were learning together. Brady was learning how to be a dog, and we were learning how to care for a young blind Brittany. None of his characteristics are in our comfort zone nor have we had experience with most of them. We started working on house training and leash walking and basic commands.

Brady mapped out his new surroundings quickly. He learned to navigate the four concrete steps from the house to the yard, and he caught on really fast where his potty spot was. He started understanding keywords like "step, watch, and this way" and was settling in nicely as our new houseguest. He'd spend a lot of time sitting in front of a window appearing to watch the world go by. I searched for toys for blind dogs online, and our search offered tennis balls and other retrieval type toys that obviously wouldn't work. I did find a company that had a ball that made noise only when it moved, and that was the ticket for our brave boy. That toy made a huge difference in Brady's trek toward dog-dom. He loved the talking ball and knew where it lived, and he'd sit under the shelf and gaze in its direction. His leash walking was actually getting worse. In the beginning he'd walk on a loose lead, but now that he was gaining more confidence, we had a Brittany teenage puller on our hands. Brady learned to jump in our laps and found joy in his daily back scratches. We found joy in hearing his deep snore from a peaceful sleep. He likes his soft bed and loves his Kong and filled bones. It had been four weeks since bringing Brady into the NBRAN family, and he had adjusted well. He was finally in a comfortable environment. Brady was learning that he didn't need to finish the entire bowl of water all at once, and he was getting the love he deserved.

Brady was adopted by a wonderful family living in Connecticut. They had a passion for loving the dogs that had chronic health problems so Brady was a perfect match for them. They have a single story home with a fenced in yard all ready for him and they were ready for Brady's arrival. Rather than going through the NBRAN transport team, we decided we'd meet his new family half way to make it easier on him. We met with them in a grassy park until Brady seemed comfortable with his new parents. They were thrilled at how steady he was. This time, he didn't go flat belly down. Brady had become a brave boy. He took his fluffy bed, his favorite talking ball, and a t-shirt his foster dad was wearing to help him settle in nicely with his new family. Brady snuggled in with his mom for their three-hour car drive home. He has adjusted well to his new surroundings and environment. He has his new yard all mapped out and can run freely and jump safely as a young Brittany should. Brady will soon undergo an eye removal surgery due to glaucoma, but we are confident he will brave through it and heal well.

People often ask us how we can let our foster dogs go because they say they'd get too attached. We have always gone into this process knowing that our job is to get these fur-babies ready for a wonderful family who will love and protect them for the rest of their lives. As soon as we send one off, we know there will be another one in need. We have foster failed twice in the past, but we will always keep our hearts and home open to helping other sweet Brittanys in the future. We will never forget our time with young Brady. He took us out of our comfort zone and taught us how to persevere but most of all, he taught us how to be brave.

# Chapter 23

## The Tale of Two Ellies

Foster name: Ellie

Foster nickname: Ellie Mae and Ellie Belle

Foster parent: Kathy Miller

Foster state: "The Peach State" – Georgia

From the time I was a child, my family had always had dogs because of my dad. I've always loved them and to me, life is not complete without a dog in it. It seemed only a natural progression for me to rescue dogs, and I often think how proud my dad must be of my endeavors. In 2014, my mentor and dear friend Nancy Cook enlisted my help because she was overwhelmed with paperwork. I spent time with her learning how each rescue dog and their situation is unique, and how each one is deserving of a loving home. In October of that year, Nancy unexpectedly passed away. I was asked if I'd consider taking Nancy's place with coordinating in Georgia with NBRAN. Out of respect for my friend,

I said yes. Since I had the gift of patience and empathy that I inherited from my dad, being a coordinator and working with dogs felt like a good fit for me. So in 2014 my journey as a state coordinator for NBRAN began.

While coordinating was a job I thought I would enjoy, I never really had a desire to foster. The idea of being a foster parent was foreign and scary. What if my own dogs didn't like the other dog? What if they didn't get along? What about behavior issues? I didn't feel trained to handle those types of situations. I've never liked the idea of being thrown into the deep end to sink or swim. Then came my first foster. I realized I was able to do it. Sometimes in life, situations come up, and we find ourselves doing things that we might never have had a desire to do but did out of sheer necessity. I was now a coordinator for NBRAN as well as a foster parent.

In January of 2018, I received a phone call the night of the National Championship game between the University of Georgia and the University of Alabama. The gentleman on the phone said, "I want you to come get this dog right now." I explained to him that it would be morning before I could get there. The next morning I arrived in Central Georgia to meet his wife. She pulled this terrified dog from a metal box that was in the back of a pick-up truck. This dog's name was Missy. The woman offered me a second female Brittany who coincidentally had the same name of Missy. I left with both Missy 1 and Missy 2. Both girls were terrified to say the least. I took them to my vet, and that is when they began their journey to forever safe and forever loved.

The two Missy's journeys took two different paths. Missy 2 found her home in Charlotte, N.C., and is living happily ever after with her new parents. Missy 1, as it turns out, was heartworm positive and needed to be spayed. She was going to be with NBRAN for a while so she could get treatment and heal. A vet tech at my local veterinarian's office wanted to adopt Missy 1. She and her boys decided to rename her Ellie. I was a little tearful over the name because my first Brittany had been Duchess Ellie whom I had lost two years prior. The vet tech that was going to adopt Ellie found that Ellie's hips were bad (hip dysplasia) so she decided to back out of the potential adoption. So the newly named Ellie was now available for adoption once again.

Ellie came home with me to finish out her heartworm treatment. I was driving her to the vet school at the University of Georgia for her injections so we could get this girl on her way to recovery. For the first time my other dogs, Jasper and Reilly, had finally found a dog they liked and welcomed Ellie into our home. She must have reminded them of Duchess Ellie that had passed away. She decided she was going to be my dog before I decided I was going to give her my whole heart. I was still grieving for Duchess Ellie and I wasn't sure my husband was on board with going back to having three dogs. Ellie, however, had already decided she was home. She quickly became my shadow dog. She would only listen to me. I knew she was completely accepted by my boys when we were driving in the car and Reilly let her use his arthritic hip for a pillow. She was still a project though. She needed to be house-broken, spayed, crate-trained and still needed work on obedience training. Ellie will chew anything soft that she can get her mouth on, and I have to watch her constantly. In addition to her hip dysplasia, her elbows on her front legs didn't ossify, so she is bow legged. Her right rear knee cap is chronically dislocated and she has an under bite. She tested negative for heartworms in October, and we were thrilled that her treatment was finally complete.

It had been a long journey with Ellie. I decided to formally adopt her on December 24, 2018. Duchess Ellie had been our Christmas puppy and it only felt right that Ellie should be the next Christmas puppy at our house. It was the perfect day to do it with the whole family at home for the holidays. We all feel like she is the dog that Duchess Ellie sent from over the Rainbow Bridge because she reminds us so much of her. She's a petite girl at 31 pounds, just like my Duchess was, and maybe that is why my boys love her so much.

Even though I initially did not want to be a foster parent, it has been a very rewarding experience. I will never forget the dogs that have graced my home, and it makes it even more special knowing that I have another Ellie to love.

# Chapter 24

## Lady

Foster name: Lady

Foster nickname: Princess

Foster parent: Sarah and Kent Kehlenbeck

Foster state: "The Hawkeye State" – Iowa

Ten years ago I fell in love with Brittanys. My husband Kent had Britts when he was growing up so we had talked about adopting one. We started following NBRAN and had come across a few beautiful dogs, but we were waiting for that special one that tugged at our hearts. One evening I ran across a senior girl that had been found wandering the streets of Indianapolis. She only weighed 18 pounds. This girl had seen rough times. Her feet showed signs of a life lived in a wire kennel and she had a broken back leg that was never treated. She was also heart worm positive. This girl needed to be loved. I talked with my husband and told him this girl was the one. Her name was Lady. She was currently being fostered by a loving woman in northern Arkansas where she would need to stay to finish out her treatment. We completed the necessary paperwork and were approved to adopt. Even though she wasn't ready to come home with us just yet, we wanted to introduce ourselves and officially meet her so on Christmas morning we did just that. We left bright and early Christmas day and made the 8-hour journey to Arkansas. There was a blizzard that day and we were driving on roads with a foot of snow. It grew dark so we found a hotel and started out again the next morning once the roads were cleared.

When we arrived, we were greeted with the barks and sounds of several dogs that were being fostered and cared for. We were introduced to the pack and immediately recognized Lady. We were in awe of her spirit and bright personality. She was playing with the younger Britts and keeping up with them like a champion. We had a great visit and knew Lady was in good hands. We said our goodbyes until we could see her again.

During the next two months we kept in touch while she recovered from her spay surgery, heart worm treatment, and began to put on weight. Finally, February 23 came and it was time to pick up our Lady. She was being transported by volunteers on the Brittany transport team and we picked her up in northern Missouri. Our girl was finally home. Our Blue Heeler Stella was a bit territorial, but Lady didn't seem to mind. She settled in nicely and continued to gain weight. She liked her yard and enjoyed spending time indoors laying on our bed and spending time on the furniture that was off limits to the dogs. Lady seemed happy, but we could tell she didn't trust us just yet. We would laugh because she'd give us dirty looks and we joked that she thought we were idiots. The truth is she had never been loved before NBRAN came in to her life. We continued to show her love and affection every day and were just enjoying having her as a part of our family.

In April we boarded the dogs because we had to leave town. When we dropped her off for boarding she still wasn't trusting us quite yet, and the bond we were hoping for still hadn't formed. We knew she just needed time. When we arrived back in town and stopped at the facility to pick up the girls, Stella came running to greet us like usual. The next thing that happened brought happy tears to our eyes. Lady saw us from across the room and ran toward us. Lady's tail was docked but, like all happy Britts, she wagged the entire back half of her body with her tail nub going 100 mph. She was so excited to see us, and we were excited too. It was at that very moment we knew she loved us. The bond was formed, and it was evident Lady was ours and we were hers.

As time went on, we added another NBRAN foster named Zeke to our pack. Lady and Zeke bonded immediately. They were inseparable. We took them to our dog park, and he paced himself so Lady could run behind him. We were never sure if Zeke was the puppy she never got to raise or just the first sweet boy who showed her love, but either way she loved him.

In early 2014, we noticed Lady wasn't herself. We took her to see our vet. It was determined that Lady had cancer. She deteriorated quickly and on January 12 2014, we helped her peacefully cross the Rainbow Bridge. It's not often you are given the chance to love a dog like Lady. She gave us her best, and we were lucky to have her in our lives. The biggest lesson we learned was how one can overcome years of abuse with love. She gave us her all, and she was one special Lady. Zeke was lost without her. It was hard for him to bond with another dog, and we lost him to cancer only 18 months later. We currently share our home with our seven-year-old Lab named Charlie. We also have a four-year-old orange and white Brittany named Duchess and a nine-month-old tri colored French Britt named Daisy. We are so grateful for NBRAN and other rescue organizations out there that give these dogs a chance at life. These sweet Brittanys make such an impact on us, and we are better for knowing them.

# Chapter 25

## The Joy of Fostering

Foster names: Bronco, Bear, Blossom, and Colt
Nicknames: Bronc, Gummy Bear, Blossom Sauce, Colty
Foster parents: Patrick, Annette, and Amanda Everson
Foster state: "The Silver State" – Nevada

Being a foster family for NBRAN has been one of the most rewarding experiences of my life. Our story starts back in 2010. Our two kids, Ryan and Amanda, had been asking us for a dog, but my husband and I had not had dogs in our lives since we were kids. We did some research online and found NBRAN. After talking with a coordinator we decided we'd start with fostering to make sure a dog would fit in with our busy lifestyle. We completed our paperwork and were soon asked to foster a five-month-old puppy named Sprinkles. Within days of him being home with us, we were smitten. Sprinkles had stolen our hearts. Our first official foster fail had happened, and we couldn't have been happier. Sprinkles, now called Bronco, was deservedly spoiled and brought us so much joy.

As the years went on, NBRAN continued to ask us to foster other dogs. My husband Pat was the lead contact on Bronco's adoption paperwork so he was the one that would always receive the calls from NBRAN. When he'd get a call about fostering, he'd always tell them no. Mind you, we did have a very hectic lifestyle with two full-time jobs and two kids with busy school activities. In 2014 he received a phone call that would change everything.

NBRAN called Pat asking him to go to a local shelter to fill out paperwork on a senior dog that had been brought in. My husband was really busy so he called me and asked me to do it. Little did he know this would change everything for our family. My daughter and I went to the shelter to fill out the paperwork and ended up bringing this senior boy home. We called him Bear. He would go on to be our second foster fail. Bear joined our pack and brought us so much love and joy until he passed away in January of 2018. NBRAN never called my husband again. I was now the lead contact and our foster journey continued.

As the years went on, my daughter Amanda and I worked to help a total of 15 dogs. Some we fostered for a week while others stayed for months. Some Brittanys were just overnight guests as they traveled to different parts of the nation to their forever home. Fostering these dogs became a thing Amanda and I did together and my husband Pat was our biggest supporter.

Over the years we fostered a nine-month-old named Misha who we told ate a couch. It turns out he was left home a lot and didn't get the proper exercise or stimulation he needed. Misha turned out to be a great dog and found a forever family living in Utah. Another dog that crossed our path was a senior named Hank who we had the privilege of transporting to his forever home in Utah. We met April who was another puppy with a lot of energy along with Skippy who found a great home in colorful Colorado. Dakota was a seven-month-old that came to us with a litter box. His owners lived in an apartment and never took him outside. Once he arrived I immediately threw that litter box away and showed him the wonders of the outdoors. He is living his best life now with a loving family that has acreage for him to run and play and use the restroom properly.

Our next houseguest came in the summer of 2017. Her name was Blossom and she was a one-year-old Brittany that had been hit by a car. She would go on to need extensive surgery, and physical therapy. My daughter Amanda was committed to her weekly physical therapy treatment and for weeks we had to carry her outside to go to the bathroom. It was certainly a labor of love. The doctors were amazed at how well she was progressing and after five long months, she was fully recovered. During those months, Blossom, Bear, and Bronco became great friends, and it was clear to us that we couldn't separate this newly-bonded pack so Blossom became foster fail number three.

With our newly formed pack we continued to foster other dogs that needed our help. Charlie was a young boy that came to us and he found a forever home in Colorado. I am grateful his new mom and I stay in touch so I get updates and get to see pictures of him growing up. After Charlie came Riley who was a senior that was found wandering the streets. He became a companion for a senior woman until he passed away in 2019.

In May of 2018 we met Colt. He had cancer and the vet only gave him a week to live. We were asked if he could stay with us for his final days. Colt reminded us so much of our sweet Bear that passed so we knew we needed to say yes. Colt only had use of three legs, and he honestly looked like he was ready to die. We brought him home and gave him the meds prescribed by the vet and were just waiting for the end. My daughter Amanda decided to give Colt the same physical therapy for his leg that she had given Blossom hoping it would make him more comfortable. She sat with him day and night. There was just one problem. Everyone forgot to tell Colt he was supposed to be dying. He made it through the week. After two weeks Colt was trying to hop around and interact with our other dogs. Blossom took a real interest in him and would bring him toys and sit with him. After three weeks, Colt started walking on all four legs. We had a dog that was clinging to life just four weeks prior, and he was now flourishing. The doctors were amazed at his blood work and all the progress he was making.

Amanda and I decided to throw Colt a birthday party for making it one month. We figured he wouldn't get to a year so we wanted to do this now while he was feeling good. We took all three dogs on a vacation to Colorado and even took them on college visits to Arizona. Colt was doing great. He made it to Christmas and in Colt's stocking was a pair of matching pajamas for him and my daughter. We all had a wonderful Christmas together. Right after the holiday Colt got really sick. We rushed him to the emergency vet and found out the cancer had taken over too much of his body, and he went on to cross the Rainbow Bridge on December 30, 2018. Our hearts were broken. Having lost Bear and Colt in the same year was a lot, but we know death is a part of life. We continued to open up our home to others like Ivey and Jazz, a bonded pair that spent the night on their way to their forever home in California. Leo was another foster that stayed with us for a few months. He was a 60-pound bundle of joy that thought he was a lap dog. He found his forever home in Los Angeles.

After many years, we continue to foster through NBRAN. It has personally been one of the greatest joys in my life and if you love dogs, I'd encourage you to give it a try. It has been a wonderful bonding experience for my family, and in the process we have been able to help many dogs. We are grateful for our time with each one and the influence they have on us. These dogs' lives are changed in such a big way through fostering and rescue but in the end, so are ours. They touch us and impact us in ways I never thought possible, and we are honored and grateful for the opportunity to serve them, to love them, and in helping them live their best lives.

www.nbran.org

info@NBRAN.org

https://www.facebook.com/NationalBrittanyRescueAdoptionNetworknbran

https://www.instagram.com/explore/tags/nationalbrittanyrescueandadoptionnetwork/